MINDFUL ABCs

Written by: Liz Medina

Illustrated by: Syad

Aa
A is for affection, a good way to show love. I show affection by raising my arms for hugs.

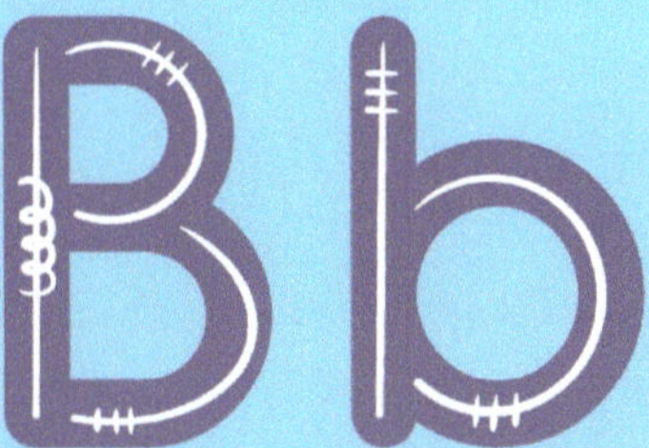

B b

B is for breathing- deep breath in, deep breath out. I do this exercise when I feel like I want to shout.

C is for communication- using words to express what I'm feeling. My grown-ups help me use my words and understand their meaning.

D d
D is for dance! A great way to get some movement. What better way than to just start groovin'?

E is for emotions. I can feel happy, sad, or excited. When I see my friends, I instantly feel delighted!

F f
F is for forgiveness. We make mistakes sometimes, it's true. I can say "I'm sorry." Now I know what *not* to do.

Gg
G is for gratitude- saying thank you for the things that I have. "Thank you for the new toy you got me for my bath!"

Hh
H is for happiness- one of my favorite emotions to feel! I get so happy when my grown-ups make my favorite meal.

Ii
I is for imagination- my brain's special power. Sometimes when I play, I imagine I'm climbing up a high tower!

Jj
J is for journaling- writing my feelings out on paper. I can write what I'm feeling so I can tell my grown-ups later.

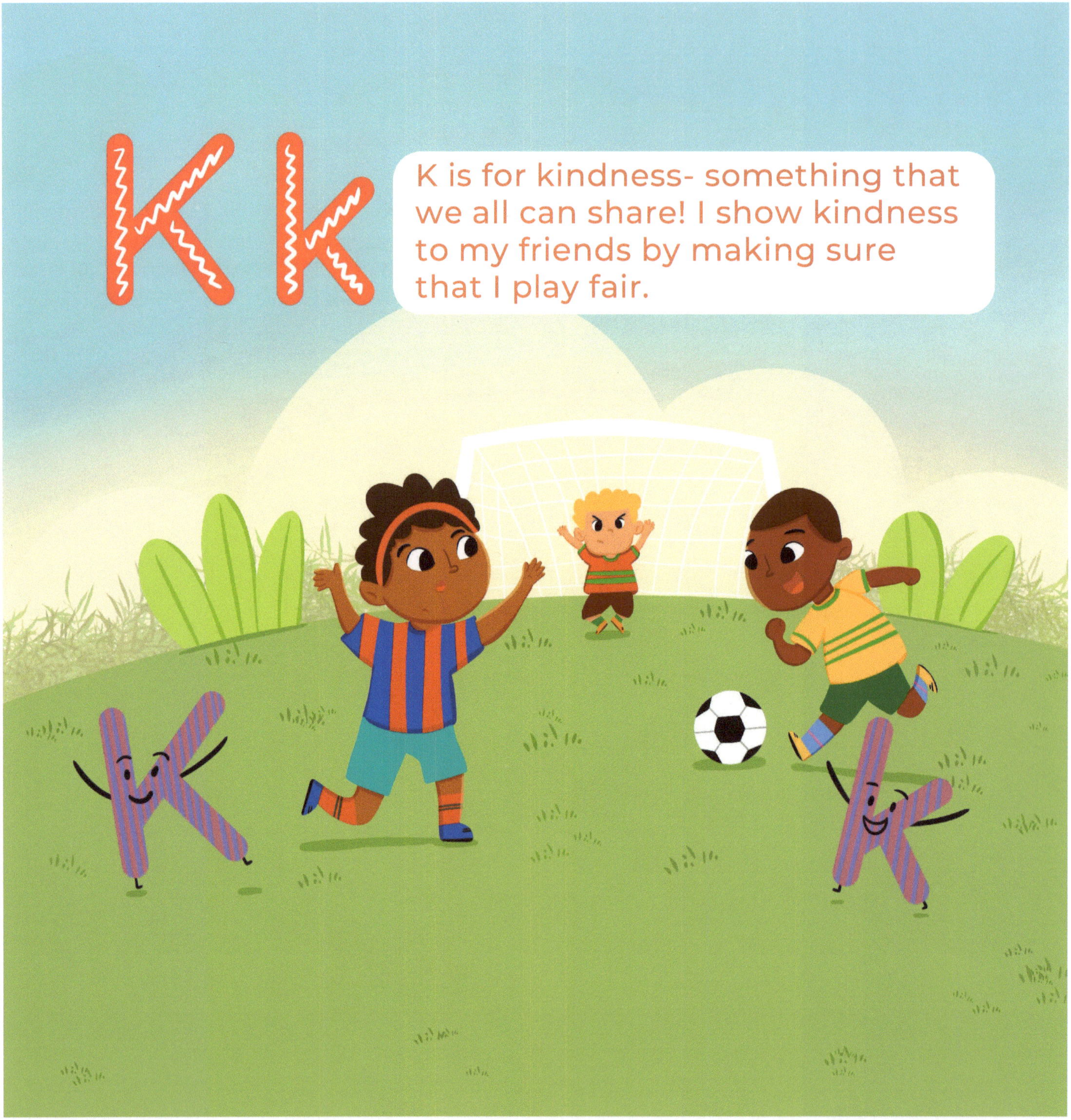

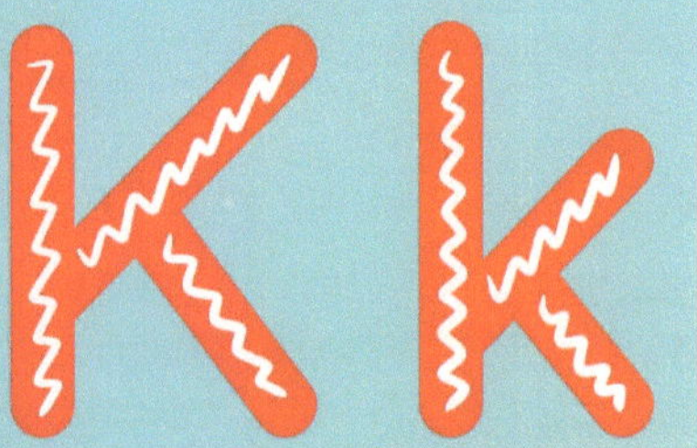

K k

K is for kindness- something that we all can share! I show kindness to my friends by making sure that I play fair.

L is for laughter- I laugh when things are funny. Flying in the air or when my grown-ups tickle my tummy.

M m
M is for mindfulness. Wind down and take your time. You can have some mindfulness by meditating before bedtime.

N n

N is for nature. I love to play outside! I like to go to the park and go down the giant slide.

O is for optimism, seeing the good in every situation. Even when things don't work out my way, I know there's always an explanation.

I CAN'T

P p
P is for positivity. Something we can share with everyone. You can spread positivity by telling someone they did a job well done.

Q is for quiet time. Sometimes, it's what our brains need. You can enjoy quiet time by finding a good book to read.
Mindful ABCs

Rr
R is my favorite, it stands for relax. My favorite way is by taking my naps.

S is for stretching- reaching high up to the sky! The sunlight on my skin feels nice, as the clouds are passing by.

T is for thank you, remember when we mentioned gratitude? Saying thank you shows someone that you are grateful for what they do.

U is for unwind, especially right before bed. My grown-ups turn off the tv and start to read to me instead.

V is for valid, meaning that my feelings are also accepted. Whether I am happy or sad, my feelings should be respected.

W w
W is for worthy. I am worthy of being loved! We are all worthy of being ourselves without being judged.

X: xoxo. Hugs and kisses from my grown-ups make everything better! Their hugs feel warm like a nice, cozy sweater.

Yy

Y is for yoga poses, there are probably tons. "Child's Pose" and "Happy Baby" are my favorite ones.

Z is for zen, feeling peace and calmness. You're doing a great job. I believe in you, I promise!

MINDFUL ABCs